About the Author

Colleen Millsteed is a poet who has been writing for forty-five years. Her first book of poetry, *Battle Angel: The Ultimate She Warrior*, was published in March 2023.

This is her second formally published book of poems.

Colleen is a born and bred Australian, using her experience of love and heartbreak as an inspiration in her writing.

Empathy of Love

Colleen Millsteed

Empathy of Love

Olympia Publishers
London

www.olympiapublishers.com
OLYMPIA PAPERBACK EDITION

A CIP catalogue record for this title is
available from the British Library.

ISBN: 978-1-80439-976-7

This is a work of fiction.
Names, characters, places and incidents originate from the writer's
imagination. Any resemblance to actual persons, living or dead, is
purely coincidental.

First Published in 2024

Olympia Publishers
Tallis House
2 Tallis Street
London
EC4Y 0AB

Printed in Great Britain

Foreword

Isn't love grand?

The butterflies in the tummy, the heart racing, the joy of feeling the love, especially the rewarding sensation of giving and sharing mutual joy, caring and support.

Our world of love captures the wonderful love of a parent for a child, which is awe-inspiring; the preciousness of the love between friends; the sensuality and bond of a life partner; the fleeting moments of love for a stranger; and many more fun-loving relationships.

Sadly, though, not all love is equal and it's not all necessarily moonshine and lace.

Love is also risky, messy, heartbreaking and soul-destroying when the end is near and after the closing of a chapter.

Then there are the toxic relationships disguised as love, such as the users and abusers, whose aim is to wreak havoc and heartbreak and there is the darkness received by domestic abuse victims. Both forms of love are crippling and detrimental to the mind, body and soul.

This collection of poems is based on my experience of love in all its shapes – the good, the bad, the crazy.

To Sir, with Love
All It Took Was That One Glance
from Across the Room

I pushed open the door to the noisy, crowded room,
As I stepped over the threshold, I came to a halt,
Suddenly, I could feel every hair on the back of my neck,
Electrified, it stood in shock, stunned from the assault.

I stood and allowed my gaze to wander over the crowd,
As I could feel both my sleeping dragons begin to stir,
They curl tighter, protective, around my scarred heart,
Then my gaze finally locks on you; who are you, sir?

I gaze into the watery depths of your sky-blue eyes,
Where I drown in your abyss, your steady gaze,
Your perfect long blonde hair frames your face,
As you capture and tame my dragons' fiery blaze.

You ensure they approve of the chemistry flowing,
Feeling like you and I are the only two in the room,
I slowly process your ruggedly handsome looks,
And feel my heart as it opens and begins to bloom.

I've lost control as my feet move of their own accord,
Following a map trail emblazoned on my scarred heart,
The X marks the spot; you are my golden precious prize,

As I realise, you are my twin flame and counterpart.

Your glorious smile is my morning sun rising at dawn,
Blazing its fiery rays around me, wrapping me tight,
Your words as you lovingly whisper them in my ear,
As I feel them shine and glitter on the moonlit night.

My heart has stopped beating, my dragons sleep,
Aware that it is you that now flows through my veins,
As I reach you, you carefully wrap me in your arms,
And my heart restarts as you unlock my chains.

I'm lost in your eyes, drowning as you soothe my life,
Calming both my dragons and black-hearted demon,
I'm now complete, realising you are no stranger to me,
You break through my shackles and give me freedom.

I am your thirst-quenching rain; you are my breeze,
You are my sun-shining day; I am your dark night,
We come together at last to join our polarities,
I am your moon orbiting, as you are my starlight.

You reach in and lovingly cup my racing bloody heart,
Soothing it as you withdraw all my pain and tears,
You turn your loving light on to defeat my darkness,
As you absorb my hatred, my anger and my fears.

I was aware from that initial first captured glance,
Where you casually stood on the far side of the room,
That my single days were done, never to be again,
One glance, I knew I was your bride and you, my groom.

Standing Strong
Against All That Would Tear Us
Asunder

To stroll along the beach once more hand in hand,
As you whisper to me your dreams of tomorrow,
My heart beats in time with yours, in happiness,
As we remove all of yesterday's sorrow.

A pause at the water's edge as we dip our toes,
Gentle waves kissing our ankles and licking our feet,
Your hand strokes my cheek in soft tenderness,
As I gaze into your eyes as, our lips gently meet.

A world of love swirls within their depths,
As I drown within your adoration,
Promises of peace and joy lay between us, unspoken,
Powerful wishes of pleasant sensation.

Our love is placed upon a pedestal,
Worshipped over the years and tenderly sculpted,
Into a barrier against the hostile outer world,
Shutting out our enemies, leaving them insulted.

Our thoughts merge into one of understanding,
Once we learn the thickness of our skin,

Standing strong, forever tethered and united,
Together, we cross our battlegrounds in an enduring win.

The length of your smile once we formed our connection,
Imprinted upon our memories, a reflection of joy,
The timbre of your voice, one that calls me home,
While the lust in my veins screams the call of a girl to her
boy.

Fingertips caressing bare naked skin,
Sensations of pleasant memories we'll take to our grave,
The gift of a hug from solid, loving arms,
Is one that we both need and one we both crave.

The solitude of a blissful night of loving in our bed,
Sheltered from the world of forbidden pain,
Soft music playing in the background as we ride the waves,
Of ecstasy and release, allowing our love to sustain.

Our connection is our armour,
Warding us from the cruel and agonising crowd,
Their turmoil that would soon tear us asunder,
Berate us, separate us, if we ever allowed.

But our commitment is strong,
Standing powerfully against the test of time,
A commitment accepting, I am yours and yours alone,
While acknowledging that you're also mine.

That Rare Connection
If You're Lucky, You'll Find It at Least Once in Your Lifetime

The connection, the instant feeling of returning home,
That infrequent ability to love unconditionally,
To stand our ground when the going gets tough,
Knowing a soul so deeply within minutes of meeting for the
first time.

The welcoming mat,
Arms hugging tightly,
Reading between the lines,
Knowing, just knowing instantly,
Eyes adoring,
Lips smiling,
Ears listening,
The rightness of two hearts beating as one.

Undefined loyalty,
Promises never to be broken.

Believing in the resounding heartbeat,
Knowing it is beating for you,
Family, but not in blood,
Authentically in truth.

That one soul that matches you perfectly,
Be it in friendship or romance,
Never to leave of their own volition.

Love,
A strong shoulder,
Who also has the courage to lean on you.

The rare connection found once in a lifetime,
Allowing you the rare ability to trust innocently,
Knowing your heart will never be trashed, broken, or discarded,
Only gently protected and forever adored.

Two authentic beings,
Meeting and melding to perfection,
Protected by their togetherness from the rest of the world,
As one, they love, nurture, strengthen and protect,
Guiding lights until the end of their time.

Heartbeats
The Pulsing World

My heart beats in time to the singer's rise and fall of her
words,
The melodically rhythm sets a course for the blood
pounding through my veins,
My inner ear can pick up the vocalist's personal heartbeat,
As both our hearts are connected by golden musical chains.

I feel her personal heart tune, beating away on autopilot,
My heartbeats choose to pulse in time,
Singing along to the words of her song,
The rhythm of multiple hearts beating in rhyme.

I feel the beats as we all sing the same chorus,
Love firming up the rat-a-tat-tats,
Each familiar pulsation radiating in my ears,
As each tether sings as it contracts and extracts.

My heart swoons at the feelings of attachment,
Hearing the joining of all those people I miss,
Far and near, their hearts pulse within me,
As every heart forwards a long-distance kiss.

The people that have passed, sadly gone from this plane,

The moment their beats stopped beating in tune,
Was the day their heartbeats buried into my soul,
And I listen to their echoes at every opportune.

If I sit in silence, I can drill down on each foreign beat,
Linked to those I choose all over the globe,
A friend, an old lover, a child, a parent,
A memory, a thought, each causes my heart to explode.

We are tethered together through our heartbeats,
Be it a single beat or a flurry of sound,
I'll know each heart intimately through their personal pulsations,
And when we're all together, the beating sounds compound.

Fall in love with someone's beautiful heartbeat,
Learn who they are through every pulsation,
Happy, sad, broken, strong, every emotion,
Gaining intimate knowledge through every palpation.

Memories with No Regrets
A Shallow Glimpse into the Past

Would it be a surprise to know you were on my mind
yesterday,
Many years have passed like water down the drain,
But I still remember every single minute,
For only a little while, then the painful memories remain.

We weren't worthy together,
Too young, too incomplete, too strong,
Substances took fast, took hold,
And it all resounded horribly wrong.

I'm sure you've often wondered over the remaining years,
The bottle of time emptying so slowly, day by day,
Where'd we end up, lost in our dreams,
Soured by the essence, the loss of the chemical way.

On this day of each year, I often revisit,
To remind myself of the lessons we learned,
Heart-wrenching, solemn dreams missed,
From others, we found the theme we yearned.

Another day, another hour, another year,
We now live in different realities,

A path we travelled when we said our goodbyes,
Setting us free to traverse our destinies.

One day in the distant future,
I'll write of my gratitude,
In the meantime, please know you have been forgiven,
Many times, over, as is my due.

Live the day in blissful ignorance,
Replacing that shut-off, unemotional heart,
The dawn will colour the land,
As the new day begins to start.

A lesson woven in between the love and the pain,
A wasted life, you'll not think that the case,
I'm glad you made the necessary decisions,
Allowing me to bow out with infinite grace.

You were not made for any other,
Another mini me thrown into the mix,
No, that may have necessitated a culling,
Sure, it would have been the quickest fix.

So long to those thoughts of yesteryear,
Until another memory rises from the ashes,
Forgotten, now the best has decayed,
A word transfixed, a look empowered, as survival clashes.

I've never held a regret,
For the future, we were left to follow,
In fact, holding on, resisting,
Would have seen us both lead a life of resounding hollow.

The Vessel of a Conundrum
As It Beats with Life

The heart is more than a blood vessel, an aorta valve,
A vein that carries life, oxygen, sustenance and hope,
It also carries love, butterflies, pain, heartache and grief,
In fact, it sometimes hurts so badly we struggle to cope.

There are days we wish the brokenness would dissolve,
Hoping the blood running through our veins,
Would dilute the pain, the misery, the hopelessness,
But it's all wishful thinking as the torment remains.

That bloody vessel can be the causation that brings us to our knees,
The crippling anxiety, the loss of appetite, the torrent of tears,
As it pounds away, without discriminating, within our chest,
Thumping harder and faster the greater our fears.

I've hurt so badly at times that I swear it rises into my throat,
Suffocating, swelling in size, determined to see me choke,
Silently beating so hard I can feel the thumps in my temples,
Positive it'll be the cause of a deadly stroke.

It aches of its own accord,
Refusing to listen to the brain,

It pounds away in a fit of grief,
Racing faster than a freight train.

It causes us so much strife,
That we've often thought of ripping it out to discard,
But it has us beat, bloody and raw,
Leaving us sobbing on the floor, horridly scarred.

It sits there innocently,
As we cycle through a love-hate relationship with it,
It plods along, not a care in the world,
Until it decides it'll race faster and then stutter, hiccup and
skip.

Just as we decide that it's not worth the pain we feel,
It'll fill with love for some stranded animal or hurt being,
We'll feel the swelling of joy in our chest,
So full of love and empathy, it is instantly freeing.

We'll forget the trouble it had recently caused,
As we feel the love, the positivity, the joy,
Never doubting that the world is a beautiful place,
Or remember that yesterday, all it did was annoy.

One moment, it's swollen, filled with love,
Then suddenly, it'll form a tiny crack,
It only takes a minute for it to shatter,
And the horrid crippling pain is suddenly back.

But without it, there'd be no life, no love,
So, we put our faith in this vessel, thumping merrily along,
Living through the pain, the grief that it sometimes feels,
I hope it'll turn things around, start beating to a happier song.

The Sealing of a Tender Kiss
Nothing More Is Necessary

His heart swells at the sight of this woman,
The one that deliciously smiles into his eyes,
She holds his hand, their fingers entwined,
And she lets out a happy and romantic sigh.

He loves this woman with his entire being,
She's all he could ever dream of finding,
He's aware of her unique preciousness,
And he plans on a ring forever binding.

He stutters in breath as he watches her glide this earth,
An angel fallen from the distance skies above,
A dove with pure white wings, floating into his universe,
Accepting and returning the productivity of love.

Her voice carries whispers only his ears can hear,
Music that adorns her breathlessly, music in which his soul
tethers,
Heartstrings entwined in the same manner as their fingers,
Ripples of ecstasy on her skin as soft as feathers.

He lays her gently by his side,
To worship her existence as is her delight,

A measure of fingertips that do roam,
Perfection, sheer perfection, is within his sight.

A single moan escapes her pretty lips,
As their souls ignite in their own glorious fire,
This is no earthly love but one made of starlight,
Filled with moonbeams and nightly desire.

A blessing to both, as they adorn their righteousness,
The beings of energy on display for each other,
Truth shining light, aiding the healing of their brokenness,
In which their love is powerful enough to smother.

Hatred does not exist within their realm,
It's impossible to feel such emotion inside their bubble,
Preciousness is the order of the day,
Disarraying all those who wish to cause them trouble.

The fullness of being when they lie together,
Is nothing but the purest of heavenly bliss,
A promise, an oath, from one to another,
Needing nothing more than the sealing of a tender kiss.

The Birthing of a New Day
Bashing Me with Its Memories

As I wander along the crisp white sands,
I remember that day, just you and I,
The memories are blasted to the forefront of my mind,
Whenever I see that gorgeous pink sky.

The clouds were formed right then, right there,
For us to gaze upon in wonder, capturing the fiery blaze,
Knowing this time would be magically
Remembered for all our following days.

It was nearly dark at first,
Then the sky began to lighten,
As you talked of the future, the possibilities,
The promises as the day began to brighten.

It was as the sun peaked shyly over the far horizon,
That you confessed your love, your dreams,
We watched as the sky turned that brilliant pink,
And we were magically highlighted within its beams.

The water reflected the beauty of Mother Nature,
Shining pristine colour across our entire world,
It was the start of a brand-new day,

And a brand-new love unfurled.

I will never look at this scene in the same way again,
Yes, it'll be beautiful every single time,
But it won't be that first, that first everything,
As it was the day you first became mine.

If I ever want to relive the gloriousness of it all,
I'd just wake up slightly before dawn,
Wander down to the sand and watch in awe,
As the new day is magically born.

Golden Memories
A Treasure Trove

Mornings, glorious mornings after the perfection of the
night,
Conversations, no small talk, deep and meaningful
knowledge,
The sensuous feeling of tickling fingertips,
Words of wisdom, words of love, both sides acknowledge.

Whispering of soul to soul, words not necessary,
Promises made, I'll forget the part about them not being
kept,
Intimate secrets traded for understanding,
Blissfully laughing, smiling, loving memories treasured and
wept.

The stolen hours, hidden away from society,
Not for long, but long enough to be cherished
As ours, never to be lost, never to be stolen,
Kept locked in safety, even after we, as one, have perished.

There are days I take out my golden memories; today would
be one,
Rifling through them like a pack of photos, freshly received,
A precious giggle escapes at a perfect moment,

Remembered in an instant, like it was just yesterday, we believed.

Some memories I hunger for, wishing they could be relived,
Others I filed in the locked heart of mine,
The best memories are savoured like a fine wine,
Polished until they're gleaming and displayed in a beautiful design.

The conversations still cause my heart to beat in excitement,
Replaying your voice over and over again in my head,
The perfect words said at the perfect time,
So, you didn't mean them, but I prefer to forget that instead.

There were many days of absolute sheer perfection,
One that stands out from the rest,
I'll never hold any regrets for that magical day,
That memory is my secret, as it was our very best.

The text messages received, shrouded in anticipation,
The excitement in your words shone through my phone,
A day knowing, we have only a few sleeps left,
Are all golden memories we lived as if we had known.

We learned so many lessons, even knowing time was not on our side,
Time may have been short, but we lived those precious hours,
Now, my memories sustain me on days like today,
Because those golden memories are magically ours.

Is There Too Much Water Under the Bridge
Or Has That Bridge Burnt Down

The years have flown, have you noticed?
It's been many, many years since we last saw each other,
Is there too much water under the bridge,
Or do we let sleeping dogs lay, rather?

I often sit and ponder,
Could life have turned out any other way?
Our choices definitely define us,
But will we ever find the courage to have our say?

Do you live with your regret,
Or even realise what it is that we missed?
Was this just our lesson to learn,
Or is this life's sad little twist?

Do you lay awake at night always wondering,
As I often do?
Unfortunately, I do think there's too much water,
In fact, I believe the bridge has been burnt, don't you?

We both realise we don't have forever and a day,
In fact, I get the feeling it won't be long and it'll all be too

late,
And yes, I'll definitely feel the regret this way,
But I've also come to terms with our fate.

I silently whisper *'I love you'* into the night,
Praying the breeze will whisk those words to you,
When you wake suddenly with no explanation,
It's my message that's disrupted your dreams to break
through.

I do hope you don't doubt how I truly feel,
Just because of the silence between us,
It was never about our love for each other,
But me knowing it's too late to cause a fuss.

One day, I'll give you my final tears,
When you're looking over me from high above,
I'll explain my silence, my distance, my fears,
And I'll send my love to you on the wings of a white dove.

I Want to Love You
But I'm a Little Bit Broken

Habits are hard to make,
But trust me, habits are even harder to break,
I've been alone for a very long time,
Tormented over my greatest mistake.

I've been convinced life is better this way,
And two decades have since flown past,
I'm stronger, happier and less lonely on my own,
I've become the ultimate successful outcast.

It helps that I'm an introvert,
Fiercely protective of my time and space,
I overwhelm quite easily,
Needing to recharge alone in a quiet place.

Does that make me crazy?
Maybe a little insane,
Some find it difficult to understand,
That being with people is an emotional drain.

It's not about you,
It was never about that,
I'll take the blame,

Yes, maybe it's me that's a brat.

I try to meet people halfway,
I understand that I'm difficult to figure out,
Independent and terribly stubborn,
But I'm made up of more than my anxiety and doubt.

I want to love you,
But I'm a little bit broken,
I'm a hot mess, I'll admit,
And not a truer word is spoken.

My heart is raw, bloodied to a pulp,
I'm not sure it even works anymore,
It's hesitant to take a risk,
As it's been beaten and shattered before.

My days of being a part of a pair
Are long gone, that boat has set sail,
Life is more peaceful when there's only one,
Less stressful and unlikely to fail.

So, forgive me,
If this habit is instilled through and through,
But I'm still a little bit broken,
No matter how much I want to love you.

Candle Lit Night
Equivalent Romance

She perfected the story of relatable effort,
Wandering light from memorial days,
The beginning, the excitement, the powerful heart,
Beating for that one that love portrays.

Starry night skies, shining over the world,
Feelings of vastness, of absolute delight,
Each pinprick is a sign of a dying star,
Signalling the importance of loving light.

Closer to home, the smell of wax,
The hypnotising allure of special flare,
The promise, the anticipation, the wishes,
Of feeling important, of welcoming care.

Jittery patterns of light and shadows,
Atmosphere of memories past,
Of magical emotions caught within its flame,
Winter was placed on hold of finer days forecast.

Enjoy the moment caught in between the shadows,
Knowing nothing is forever, but memories will do,
Mindfully prepare for the end of time,

Leaving you at peace with a future breakthrough.

Leave tomorrow where it belongs,
Turn the flickering light into pure joy,
Welcome the lesson as it needs to run,
Without time on her side, she'll not allow it to destroy.

All is as it should be,
The flickering flame to reminisce,
Love as deeply as she can,
The emotions caught in one spellbinding kiss.

His Gaze upon Her Skin
Was All It Took

She knocked on a friend's door, looking for company,
She was in luck as the door opened wide, inviting her in,
She was led to the back verandah, where others were waiting,
The centre of attention, as she stepped outside, gazes on her
skin.

Shock ripples through her as she spies that perfect set of
eyes,
Black slicked-back hair and the deepest, brightest gaze,
Tingles shot through from the tip of her toes to the tip of her
nose,
Electric shocks running the blood in her veins ablaze.

Hours of flirty giggles and come hitherto smiles,
As they each sipped their Dutch courage, gaining strength,
They sneak out for a welcome walk alone,
Knowing they were both on the same glorious wavelength.

As they hit the sand, he takes her hand,
Suggesting a midnight swim,
Off with the jeans and shirt, a race into the waves,
Finding they were nothing more than a tangle of limbs.

They tasted their first salty kiss,
And magic began to bloom around them this night,
As they dashed, giggling and happily, back to hit the shower,
To cleanse the salt and sand from each other in delight.

A night remembered often, along with the numerous replays
They endeavoured to enjoy, over the next few years,
Until things began to change, horridly so,
And the end then followed with a torrid of endless tears.

A Heart Full of Hope
Knowing That We Will Meet Again

My memories of you are always at the very forefront of my mind,
All those years that we laughed, loved, supported and cared,
And in those years there are some of the happiest times of my life,
Which I constantly relive, especially during the times I'm scared.

We were there for each other, holding tight in a metaphorical hug,
You'd give me solemn advice when I was falling apart and sad,
Although during those times, you, too, were uncertain about life,
You slipped into my heart, ignoring the fact it was armour-clad.

Nothing was ever too much and there were times you put me first,
My most treasured memory was you forgiving my greatest mistake,
As I held on tight through the rough seas, leaning on your shoulder,

And you wrapped me in your loving arms, soothing my heartbreak.

On the days that I thought I'd never survive, you encouraged me,
And when I was happy and giggling in glee, you laughed too,
During my nightmares, you were my knight in shining armour,
Congratulating me when I found my strength and pulled through.

You welcomed me in from the cold and sheltered me when I was in need,
During the heat, you passionately stood by my side, sword in hand,
As the two of us fought my demons, scarring them as they fled,
I was never alone; I never had to run; you helped me take a stand.

Do you remember those few precious days that were just for us?
Where we hid from the world, soaking up the peace and quiet,
Where there was no longer one, no longer a solo soldier fighting,
But two, ready to take on the entire world, willing to start a riot.

I can hear your encouraging and loving words whispered in my ears,

Because you never doubted me, never gave up on my inner strength,
There were days I felt I was a coward, unworthy of you, of the world,
It was all you working tirelessly to get me on the same wavelength.

Never a harsh word between us, you ignited my compassion, my love,
One of the proudest moments of my life, giving to you all you needed,
When I was able to return the support, convince you that you're worthy,
To insist you stand tall, head held high, watching as you succeeded.

There were times you were your own worst enemy, conceding defeat,
Swamped in the darkest corners of your torturous and bleeding heart,
Caging your soul, locking it behind those hideous metal bars, chained,
It'd take my all to coach you back into the light, insisting on a fresh start.

Then, one unexpected day, you were gone, ripped violently from my world,
There'll never be another capable of filling that devastating hole in my chest,
But I take comfort knowing that we will never end; there'll always be an us,

You, the other half of my soul, the protector of my heart, were the very best.

I wait for that day, knowing it'll show up at just precisely the right time,
Knowing that you, too, are waiting, biding your time on the orbital plane,
Both anticipating our reunion, our connection too strong to ever die,
I take great comfort in knowing that one day, my friend, we'll meet again.

She Needed Love
Her Weakness Would Be Her
Demise

I watch her as she breaks, devastated,
And there it is, during this difficult time,
An innate ability to understand who she is,
And what it is that makes her a paradigm.

I love her heart, that wonderful goodness,
No, that's not true, it's a beautiful heart,
But one that has been burned, tortured
Until she hides, looking for a fresh start.

She was treated brutally until she finally broke,
All because she thought she needed love,
I cried at the unfairness, the horrid pain,
She was dealt a bad hand when push came to shove.

It was her horrid childhood from the start,
And the heartbreak of lovers that cheat,
That turned her into a tortured beast,
So, she'd never ever again bow to defeat.

She now refuses to take hell from anyone,
As she weaves in and out through her day,

She no longer has the ability to feel fear,
Head held high regardless of all they say.

She holds her closest secret to her chest,
That one lonely fear she cannot put to rest,
The fear of ending up solely on her own,
Feeling she'd always be alone, she stressed.

This fear's her weakness, her possible demise,
I fear it may even be her total self-destruction,
I try to tell her she's stronger than her fear,
That it's her final hurdle, her final obstruction.

She is a badass woman, the strongest yet,
I struggle to convince her of this actual fact,
She feels she cannot survive without love,
While sacrificing herself, trying to distract.

I fear she will wither away slowly in the process
Of finding the love she's convinced she needs,
Will she be the cause of her own destruction,
As she opens her heart and allows it to bleed?

Fleetingly Perfect Happiness Worth Living a Lifetime to Experience Even Just Once

You placed a crown upon my head on this very day,
My face graced a smile that made my eyes shine,
On a beach of pure white sand and pure blue seas,
The sun was shining; both were blessed on a day so fine.

Happiness was bliss, I couldn't have asked for more,
My time had finally arrived and the world was mine,
White sand, bare feet, black jeans and silver rings,
A palm tree, bending in the wind, our glorious shrine.

It had been twenty years since I'd felt such happiness,
A day that was both pivotal and importance combined,
I watched as you cried in joy; the truth finally revealed,
We had both waited for ever so long for just this sign.

That memory is tucked into my heart, never forgotten,
Like it all happened just yesterday, our hands entwine,
Happiness this pure doesn't come around that often,
So, I give way to my grief today. Is it any wonder I pine?

Our day was different combinations of black and white,
It was so typically us, unspoken but organised by design,

You and your best friend both draped from head to toe
In the blackness of your heart, shrivelled and evil malign.

I learned bitterly that ecstatic happiness is way too high,
The fall back to earth is a sudden drop, not a slow decline,
If ever given the choice, I'd live happily that day again,
Because that type of happiness, even for a day, is divine.

Nineteen years have passed since, do you often wonder
As I do, if we individually attempted to go out and find?
Did you feel happiness once again as pure as that day,
Or, like me, you knew our day would forever outshine?

Never Let Them Go
That's My Advice for What It's Worth

We have all heard the stories of angels,
The fairy tales that we grew up hearing,
But would you believe if you were told,
The tales are true, as you were fearing.

Of all the stories and the angels' glories,
My favourite would be a toss-up of two,
First, the tale of the pure white angels,
With their wings tucked in, out of view.

The second favourite, now let me see,
That would be those poor fallen souls,
The fallen angels, with their wings torn,
Those that believed in minor loopholes.

Both sets of angels look like you and me,
Those with closed hearts, locked minds,
Will not understand or even recognise,
These unique beings as angel kind.

Look closely; those who are often feared,
The groups that often receive your scorn,

They may have fallen, but please believe,
They're love and strength, although torn.

Those that have so little but still give all,
Those that only offer unconditional love,
Those that try as they might, never fit in,
Their home is not here; it's up there above.

They are the most precious of beings,
Often cast as the outsiders, the freaks,
The loners, the introverts and the lonely,
Those shy individuals too scared to speak.

It's those beings constantly overlooked,
The quietly abused, those we all trample,
The tormented, the tortured, are the same,
They are the ones terrorised, as an example.

Think twice next time you see a poor soul,
And if you are fortunate enough to find,
Make the effort to befriend this outcast,
Take the time to listen sincerely, be kind.

If your offer of friendship is to be accepted,
Ensure you smile happily as you say hello,
I would suggest you treasure them dearly,
And find a way to never let an angel go.

You Are My Heart
You Are the Best Thing to Ever Happen to Me

My world would be incomplete without you,
My days would be cold without your smile,
My house empty without your footsteps,
Your presence makes my life worthwhile.

My ears would be deaf without your laughter,
Your conversations have now become my song,
Your hugs are my haven, my safe place,
Your happiness is my goal; it's where I belong.

Your safety is paramount to my peacefulness,
Knowing you are at peace is my blessing,
Seeing you sprout your wings to fly free,
Your individuality is growing and progressing.

My heart would be bloody without your joy,
I would be a shell of the person I have become,
My strength would be nothing without you,
You're the best thing to happen to me, my son.

Life would not be worth living without you here,
I couldn't bear the thought of us being apart,
Experiencing your joys, sadness and small wins
Are our precious memories, as you are my heart.

Love at First Write
A Modern-Day Love Story

We live in a different world these days,
A world where you're more likely to meet,
Online, a dating site, even social media or,
Chat rooms, rather than a meet and greet.

So, hang awhile and let me tell you a story,
It's not what you think, love at first sight,
It all occurred online, a creative platform,
Making it a modern-day, love at first write.

I uploaded and published a poem one day,
Where I later found this perfect comment,
Beautifully written, unique and encouraging,
I read between the lines what he really meant.

I responded with kindness and gratitude,
Maybe slipped in a double-edged innuendo,
My next poem was ready to be published,
The next comment I've kept as a memento.

Light-hearted banter, both back and forth,
Until one comment slammed into my heart,
There it lodged hard, as content as can be,

Causing my heart to swell and love to start.

Then, there was silence; I became concerned,
Convinced I'd gone and said something wrong,
I checked and checked, but not a word to see,
I just wanted to see that one name I longed.

I wrote a poem with a simple secret message,
And saw a beautiful response the very next day,
I took my courage and asked to speak off-site,
Hoping and praying I wasn't chasing them away.

From there, we went from strength to strength,
So, I will say it again: it was no love at first sight,
It all happened in this the modern-day world,
It was through words, becoming love at first write.

If I Could Tell You I Love You Just One More Time
I Would Give My All for That One Last Chance

If I ever had even a small chance in life,
To hold you and tell you once more,
That my love expands the eternal sky,
Ghostly rainbows showing all I adore.

I would give up every day I had left on earth,
To climb the one-way staircase to above,
Even if only given one day with you,
I would shower you with my adoring love.

You were my Twin Flame, my other side,
And I will never know a love like this again,
You were taken from me way too soon,
And I've struggled with decades of pain.

You were always an angel, one without wings,
The very essence of my soul's mate,
I've bottled all the memories in gold,
Only pouring through them on special dates.

I look forward to the time that'll be ours,
One day, I, too, will grow my wings,
The years have taken their toll,
But I know that true love always wins.

So, my handsome Angel sitting up high,
I can always feel you watching from above,
Please know that all through the years past,
My heart is full, for you, of abundant love.

Until then, my Twin Flame – we will meet again.

Dare to Swim
Take the Time to Ponder

Walk with her awhile, go join her,
Talk with her as you wander,
Take the time before to decide,
Stop, think and heavily ponder.

You are, of course, welcome,
To join her on her journey,
But weigh up the pros and cons,
And decide if you are worthy.

Know this upfront, so be sure to listen,
There's nothing casual about her love,
She loves hard and she loves forever,
Make sure you're okay with the above.

When she loves, you'll burn in her fire,
Singed by her passion, set alight,
Blissfully floating on cloud nine,
Sleeping in her dreams every night.

When she laughs, you'll stop, listen,
Bathing in her music willingly,
Your smile will light up your face,

Causing her heart to beat thrillingly.

When she cries, you'll know her pain,
As you will dance within her storms,
Torrents of tears embraced,
As the dam dries and reforms.

When you kiss, you'll feel her love,
You'll drown in her soul happily,
You'll hesitate to come up for air,
The fire ignited and burning rapidly.

Think carefully and be totally sure,
As her depths are littered with debris,
From the ruins of those who struggled,
Navigating her currents to any degree.

The waters surrounding her spirit,
Are a graveyard of those passed,
Their crime, the depth of their love,
Being too shallow to ever last.

Again, she forewarns, so take heed,
Think hard, do not act on a whim,
Do not set foot in her ocean,
Unless you are ready to swim.

Intimacy at Its Finest
I Crave This Amazing Connection

When you think of intimacy,
I'm guessing you think only of sex,
While you wouldn't, in theory, be wrong,
I crave that which comes next.

Intimacy is letting someone inside,
To nestle deep within your heart,
It's whispering together late at night,
And making eye gazing an art.

Intimacy is crying on each other's shoulders,
And honouring each other's tears,
It's talking about your deepest pain,
And sharing all your secret fears.

Intimacy is sharing life stories,
Talking about the past and growing up,
Going places that hold shameful memories,
Of all your past hiccups.

Intimacy is exchanging energy,
Feeling the other without so much as a touch,
Being in tune to each emotion,

Knowing their moods as such.

Intimacy is baring your soul,
Even when you are so afraid,
Knowing and trusting it will be protected,
While wearing your heart on full display.

Love Is Not Enough
There Is So Much More That Is Necessary

I have been asked the question,
Is love enough, yes or no?
I can honestly tell you,
I learned firsthand; you know.

There is so much more needed.
For a relationship to last,
There's respect for each other,
And honesty about the past.

Compromise is hugely important,
Especially if it is one-sided,
There's give and take, too,
If just taking, it's terribly misguided.

Compatibility is a key to love,
Without it, there will be issues,
Listen quietly and respectfully to each other,
Or you're going to need tissues.

These are just some examples.
Of traits needed over and above,

There are many more,
That are needed, other than love.

No, love is definitely not enough,
For your relationship to survive,
You'll need so much more,
For you both to stay and thrive.

It's Hard to Say Goodbye
Let Them Go with Grace – Their
Job Is Done

We win, we lose, we start, we stop,
We battle and struggle awhile,
Decipher the lessons you've learned,
In your experiences and trials.

Every person that we meet,
Is there for a particular reason,
They will enter your life,
Some staying for years, others just a season.

It's all dependent on your needs,
Don't mistake this as your desire,
As they are both totally different,
Needs, not want, are what you require.

People will be embedded in your life,
Until you discover and learn why,
Then they'll waltz back out again,
At times, without so much as a goodbye.

There's no point in fighting this,
It's important you let them go,

They've done what they come for,
And deep in your heart, you know.

Mourn them, if need be,
Spend the time you need to cry,
Heal your shattered heart,
Feel each emotion that applies.

Do not struggle, just accept,
This is not the time to deny,
Be strong, be brave and smile,
Send them off with a wave goodbye.

An Instruction Manual for Your Woman When She's Had a Hard Day
Be Her Perfect Shoulder to Cry On

When your woman walks in the door,
After a horribly hard day,
The importance is on how you react,
To help her feel okay.

She's often just looking for an ear,
A strong shoulder for her tears,
Hold her close, don't say a word,
Silently listen to her fears.

You don't need the answers,
She doesn't expect you to know,
She doesn't need it fixed,
Just your shoulder when she's low.

Listen to her talk,
Let her freely cry,
Gently rub her back,
While she tells you why.

Turn on the music,
Listen to her favourite song,
Unsure of what to say? Then, quietly hold her,
This way, you can't go wrong.

She, too, will return the favour,
On your hard-won days,
Lay your head on her shoulder,
And she'll listen in the same way.

If Wishes Were...
I Would Feel Blessed

If wishes were fishes,
Oceans would be teeming,
If wishes were kisses,
I'd believe I was dreaming.

If wishes were dreams,
I'd sleep through the day,
If wishes were loving,
I'd be feeling okay.

If wishes could travel,
I'd be there with you,
If wishes were sensual,
I'd give more than a few.

If wishes were coins,
I'd be extremely rich,
If wishes were lucky,
I'd sew in every stitch.

If wishes were happy,
I'd smile all day through,
If wishes were true,

I'd never be blue.

If wishes were easy,
I'd have all I need,
If wishes were magic,
I know I'd succeed.

If wishes came true,
I'd be somewhere new,
If wishes time travelled,
I'll come and find you!

To My Past, from Your Future
Dance with Me

She'd locked her door to her tower,
And throw away the key,
Sheltering from the pain inside,
Pushing away those who'd set her free.

Until she discovered a world where she may belong!

She discovered a loving kindred spirit,
Only he is living in her past,
Together with a wish to be in his arms
For a dance or two at last.

For the pleasure of a simple kiss, she'll stand strong!

She lives patiently in his future,
Knowing it's for his love, she waits,
Eventually, her past will catch her,
Regardless of how long it takes.

When she wishes for forever, she knows he'll understand!

She doesn't care if she gets lost in her past,
Knowing time is precious, not to be taken lightly,

So darling, will you dance to these songs with me,
While wrapping me in your arms and holding tightly?

When the past and the future collides, she'll find her loving
man!

You Have My Gratitude
Was It My Heart You Broke or My Ego

After the terrible week I've had this week,
I decided to concentrate on my gratitude,
And it got me seriously thinking of you,
The guys I have loved with any magnitude.

The bulk of you only lasted a few months,
Or for some, maybe even a year or two,
When we break, I've often wondered,
Was it my heart you broke or my ego too?

I start to question, did I love you,
And I can quickly answer yes, it was true,
It hurt immensely when we did finally part,
And for a short period, I was feeling blue.

Delving deeper, I realised it was never our love,
That I was often searching high and low for,
It was never that earth-shattering, deep-seated,
Powerful heart-stopping love that I adore.

So, for you, I share my deepest gratitude,
You saved me from a dissatisfied love affair,

We were one that didn't sustain us for long,
Leaving me free to find love elsewhere.

I'm grateful for the lessons you taught me,
Especially the one where I knew to hold out,
Stay single until that one special soul,
Buries so deep in my heart, there's no doubt.

So, to all those guys who up and left me,
Please know I'm so very grateful to you,
Each of you were but a steppingstone,
To the one I'll love the rest of my days through.

On a Bed of Moss
A Meeting to Remember

I pulled into the empty, forsaken parking lot,
Surrounded by beauty, bird songs and trees,
The harmony of nature forever calling to me,
Singing ever so seductively on the breeze.

I entered the rainforest trail hesitantly,
My stomach full of nervous butterflies,
My heart swollen and stuck in my throat,
A bright smile on my face and in my eyes.

I meander slowly through the bush trails,
Heading towards our secret meeting place,
As I get closer, I begin to speed up my steps,
Desperate to cast my eyes on your face.

There you are, waiting patiently for me,
My last steps rushed as I dived into your arms,
I raise my face to look up at you with anticipation,
For that first kiss, as you hold me in your palms.

It was as sweet as I had imagined it to be,
Full of all our feelings of pent-up love and lust,
You suddenly break away from my lips to trail

Kisses on my neck, almost causing me to combust.

You gently lay me down on a soft bed of moss,
Asking a question with your eyes, hands still,
Then, you slowly remove the barriers between us,
The touching of our bare skin is a magical thrill.

Your gentle touch explores me from head to toe,
As you begin to make love to me ever so lovingly,
You've blown my mind, I'm incoherent,
Every nerve alive as you touch me seductively.

I lay there in your arms, totally and fully sated,
You fulfilled my every wish, my every desire,
I travelled up and over a glorious wave of pleasure,
As your touch, your love, set my body on fire.

I gracefully stretch my body, cuddling in closer,
I can still feel tiny shivers up and down my spine,
I gradually open my eyes and stare at the ceiling,
Realising it was a dream. Oh, but a dream so divine!

Once Black and White
Now, the Colours Are Starting to
Shine Once Again

It has now been almost two decades long,
I've lived here in a world of black and white,
The colour had been leeched from my life,
I looked through eyes that saw dark, not light.

My body alive with blood that ran black,
Pumped non-stop by a heart-grown dark,
Heightened solid black walls protecting it,
Not much in my life that caused a spark.

My thoughts were restricted, closed off,
My world allowed to grow extra small,
Only two special souls given free access,
The rest of the world is not allowed in at all.

But lately, I've begun noticing the sunrises,
As it climbs the world in all its stunning glory,
Bright colours slowly fading in its wake,
Colourful regardless of its past life story.

I glanced outside today and noticed in delight,
Bright red flowers of the magnificent flame tree,

Advertising Christmas is just around the corner,
I'm allowing colour in and setting the dark free.

The colour has slowly been leeching in unnoticed,
Life is suddenly filled with glorious possibilities,
Chambers of my heart are slowly unlocking,
Walls being dismantled, destroying its disabilities.

I'm beginning to smile and say yes to life again,
My heart is relearning what it's like to skip a beat,
My mind is reinventing daydreams once more,
I'm loving the dance finding its way back to my feet.

Anticipation is wondrously building deep inside,
New possibilities are now given second chances,
There is far less darkness surrounding me,
Bright, shining new colours make their advances.

Locked and Double Walled
The Tying up of Loose Ends

At times, you are so often on my mind,
I'm then left to wonder where you are,
I question whether you are finally happy,
While always loving you from afar.

It's unbelievable after all these years,
I'm finally letting my wounded heart heal,
I think I'm ready to close our book,
Flaunting my strength as I work on how I feel.

We possibly still have a chapter or two left,
That's if I consider tying up that loose end,
Or maybe I'll let sleeping dogs lie after all,
Possibly the cost is more than I want to spend.

We will continue to replay our story,
I've got my memories, good and bad,
I may stop in to visit occasionally,
But not enough to start feeling sad.

All these very long years, I've hesitated,
To visit you in my deep, darkened heart,
To utter that final dreadful word goodbye,

Then section off my heart to keep us apart.

I was confident, in fact, that I'd never be ready,
I believed I couldn't bear it if I severed our last tie,
My heart linked directly into your heart by a fine line,
All I need to do is snip that line and say my goodbye.

I'm so sorry, as I know we promised forever,
Sadly, you took that promise and threw it all south,
I've held onto us safely for as long as I could,
It's almost time to say the words from my mouth.

I need to pack, you and my leftover love, away now,
In my heart, pushed to the very back, a wall was installed,
There, you'll stay for my forever; it's the best I can do,
A heavily scarred, tiny pocket, locked and double-walled.

Two Hearts
In Total Sync

Gallons of water,
Can't stop two hearts,
That beat as one!

Do you feel me?
As I wrap my arms,
Around you,
Holding you close.

Feel my admiration,
As I push my hands,
Up under your shirt,
To feel your bare skin.

My fingers moving
Up your spine,
I feel a shiver
Through my
Fingertips.

I gaze up at you,
Adoringly,
As you lower your

Lips to mine.

Our first kiss,
As sweet
As I dreamed,
Wanting for more.

Your skin heats
Under my hands,
As they continue
To roam,
To explore.

The desire
To know,
Every inch
Of you.

Can you feel me?
Across the miles,
As my hands wander,
Learning, loving,
Now you are mine.

An Invite to the Universe
Our Producer and Director

I'm sending through an invite,
To take that prized front-row seat,
Watch as the production plays out,
Starring two actors destined to meet.

Feel the tension swirling through the air,
The audience is swept up in emotions
Being played out on the world stage,
Partly across miles and miles of ocean.

The background music begins to build,
As the separated couple wish and yearn,
Taking the time they've been given,
To talk, laugh, open their hearts and learn.

The script has not yet been completed,
The production is missing an ending,
Hence, the invite was sent through to you,
Your thoughts and advice are still pending.

They will need you to intervene,
Remove all obstacles in their way,
The audience holds their breath,

Waiting for you to have your say.

It's understandable you need time,
There's no rush as these two dance,
Learning, listening, growing closer,
They are only asking for a chance.

They are fully prepared to accept,
The consequences that arise,
If you choose to accept their invite,
Of course, there's a lot to organise.

I will just leave the invite right here,
For you to pick up and process at will,
I trust you'll take the wisest path,
And honour them with your goodwill.

That Elusive Human Connection
That Rare Connection in My Life

I'm your classic introvert, struggling with that necessary
human connection,
I'm socially awkward and try to steer clear of parties and
crowds,
I attend all my theatre productions and music concerts alone,
Only my boys' intrusion on my life is allowed.

I detest small talk in any way, shape, or form,
Seeing it for the time waster and connection killer that it is,
The asking of questions you hope remain unanswered,
I don't see the sense or want to play the game to any of this.

I will happily take a week's leave from my employment,
And spend that entire week home on my own,
Not opening my front door even once during that time,
And treasuring my own space, enjoying being alone.

Ten years, I've now lived in this large city,
Not made even one friend in all those years,
I don't have much need for a string of people in my life,
I make do and only need my small family, it appears.

Then, along will come that beautiful human soul,

Where I will instantly connect to their bright, shining light,
That pushes aside my darkness my walls and opens my heart,
That soul that slots in beside me as if it's their right.

This is an extremely rare occurrence, but when it does connect,
There's this synchronicity that occurs outside of my control,
It's the universe ensuring I don't push that one individual away,
That one person that's going to become important to my soul.

I've learned to listen to the universe to take heed when I do meet,
That one individual that has instant access to my closed-off heart,
Whether they be meant as a temporary lover, a long-term friend,
Or the next soul that blesses my life my heart with love from the start.

When I do feel the snap of that instant bond, that instant connection,
I know I have found a beautiful kindred spirit, an equally vulnerable being,
One that will show me their brutally honest soul, laying their shame at my door,
Knowing I will perform the same for them, almost a mirror image, it's so freeing.

That connection that will move forward performing miracles,

Removing obstacles that we see as an unmovable brick wall,
Whether that be the difference in a culture or the spanning of age,
The insurmountable miles between you, any possibilities known to stall.

Don't get me wrong, any connection that's meant to click,
Doesn't mean it will be necessarily easy, even if right,
That special rare occurrence of a deep-seated connection,
You will both need to put in the hard yards and take up the fight.

To You Today and Always
To You, Especially Today

Happy Birthday, Happy Birthday to you,
Happy Birthday to my darling heart,
I love you always, for all of eternity,
I love you even when we are apart.

Wherever you are, I hope you are happy,
Surrounded by special people who care,
Spoiling you today, especially today,
This momentous date that with you, they share.

You are forever in my loving thoughts,
On days like today, you are even more,
I must believe life has been good,
Or has it made you even up the score?

I wish you many lifelong blessings,
To be showered upon you every day,
Love, light and happiness for you,
All good, no bad, to come your way.

I often wonder if you ever did find,
The elusive you've been searching for,
I don't believe you ever knew what

It was that you wanted to score.

Tell me just once, were there any regrets?
Were you sorry for the part you played?
If you could reverse your choices,
Would you be any happier today?

Happy birthday, my love, my heart,
Birthdays are a good day for reflecting,
The past, the present and the future,
Are there any areas you may be neglecting?

For the last time today, Happy Birthday,
I give the freedom of my thoughts today,
I remember, I reminisce, I dwell, I love,
But tomorrow, I'll pack my thoughts away.

I Remember You
Our Memories Are Still Alive and Well

I wake in the morning,
Stretching out lazily,
It's a fresh new day,
Let's start it happily.

Then I remember you.

I move about my day,
Through the motion
Of day-to-day living,
I'm no longer broken.

Then I remember you.

At the end of the day,
I lie in bed dreaming,
Thinking about life,
My smile is beaming.

Then I remember you.

My mood rises and falls.

With my thoughts,
Happy day to day,
Generally, on course.

Then I remember you.

I am totally fine until
You enter my mind.
I brush you aside,
But you refuse to hide.

Then I remember you.

What Love Is About
Two People and Their Feelings

I never really thought until now,
What love is all about,
Two people and their emotions,
Amicably sorting problems out.

Two people sticking together,
Daily, through thick or thin,
Hanging on during tough times,
Until happiness begins to win.

Making their mundane lives,
Be a blessing in disguise,
Even the boring routines,
Are exciting in their eyes.

It is dreaming of a future,
That fairy tales do come true,
Knowing they'll never be alone,
As there will always be two.

It's when the sun shines,
Even on stormy cloudy days,
When they see their partner,

As their love's sunshine rays.

During bad and stressful times,
One hug can make it right,
Confident in relaying secrets,
Knowing they'll guard them tight.

Waking next to each other,
Starts the day off with glee,
Knowing they are not bound,
Together, they're totally free.

A single hug and a sweet kiss,
Understood by their loving heart,
They can talk about anything,
As it has been from the start.

It's the trust that each show,
And saying how much they care,
Knowing when they need a shoulder,
The others will always be there.

Passion
Is It Possible to Love Too Much

Is it possible to love too much,
For passion to burn too hot?
There's pros and cons attached,
But is it too much, too hot, or not?

Have you experienced this type of love,
Where you love as hard as you fight?
There is no middle ground,
But does it make it wrong or right?

You can spend your nights loving,
And it doesn't get much better than this,
But then your days are furious and fierce,
The very opposite of your night-time bliss.

They say it's a fine line between love and hate,
Or is it the burning passion calling?
The two sides of the same coin,
Can be either heaven or downright appalling.

Do you leave due to the fighting,
Or stay because the loving is amazing?
To go would be the ultimate sacrifice,

But you'd find the peace you've been craving.

The years then tick on by,
Are you living or just surviving?
Each dreary day is the same,
Due to the passion you've been depriving.

Is it possible to love too much,
For passion to burn too hot?
Better to have loved and lost,
Than to never have that shot!

One Woman's Life
Good Luck

All my life, I've been shy, quiet and usually on my own,
From this, I've developed the skill of watching the world go
around,
Watching the trials and tribulations of other lives that unfold
before me,
And I've been fascinated with this one woman's life, with all
its ups and downs.

I've watched this woman struggle with her life in the big city,
So different to what she's used to, as she is from a different
land,
Her daily routine is made up of looking after her children and
working,
As a long-term single mother who takes her responsibilities
in hand.

She knows no one in her new world and has no help of any
kind,
But that's not unusual as she's always gone it alone,
For so long, in fact, that she no longer knows how to ask for
help,
But she's happy with her lot in life as it's all she's ever
known.

City life is certainly a struggle and people seem to be from another planet,
They won't give her the time of day and she has no one to call a friend,
But again, she has lived alone so long that she doesn't let that stop her,
And she gets through each day, ensuring her children's happiness knows no end.

Then, I watched as this woman met someone who was to become the light of her life,
I watched her smile widen and her life blossom into full bloom,
This man now walks beside her and she is no longer alone,
I was ecstatic to see this woman grow and find the courage to reach for the moon.

Over the months, this woman began to shine and glow with happiness,
As she came into her own, she found love and peace in this place she now calls home,
Her smile became brighter daily; her happiness shone through,
And her children benefited from this larger-than-life romance that had grown.

Suddenly, where there was already a loving family living under one roof,
There was an additional person included in its fold,
That not only made that family more loving and content,
But instilled magic in their lives and turned it all into gold.

I was honoured to have witnessed this transformation,
And thankful for such a wonderful outcome for this woman
and her family,
The magic that life could visit on them when true love was
found,
And I also knew this wasn't an everyday occurrence, but a
true miracle abound.

But then I watched it slowly disintegrate as this woman's
smile started to turn upside down,
As she discovered that all she had been led to believe,
Was maybe nothing more than an illusion and wishful
thinking,
And I watched as her smile turned into a frown.

It seems that the true happiness that was found under her
roof,
Was simply that, a secret that couldn't survive outside the
door,
Although she had opened herself up, sharing all that she was
and all that she'd known,
Sharing her love, her body, her dreams, her family and even
her home.

This new passion, her new life, her new love, had a life of his
own,
In which he didn't wish her to share, a part of him that didn't
have a space for her to be,
His life, his home and his family were to be kept as a separate
entity,
For which she was not to be included and for which she was
never to see.

Sadly, I watched this woman as the realisation seeped in,
That her new life, her new love, was possibly an illusion and nothing more than a vivid dream,
I watched as she discovered that she obviously wasn't worthy, not nearly good enough,
To receive in the same way as she had given, or so it now seemed.

I saw this woman start to fade and melt back into her solitude,
To again accept her lot in life, to know she was always to be kept in the background,
To be locked away in secret and only to be taken out when there was no one around,
As her love must be ashamed of her and her family, or so she'd found.

I found myself crying to sleep on her behalf,
As I watched her struggle and hold it together with her amazing strength,
She crawled back into herself and took time out, then arose once again,
To carry on doing her duty, to hide her hurt and pain at great length.

I can only hope and pray that for this woman,
To find that her dreams have only gone astray,
A small setback, a dent as such and she'll successfully gather them back in,
And build them back up to strive and survive another day.

Our Tree
Is Dying

Survey the bush as you walk forward,
Pick out the tree that looks the most stressed,
Notice the leaves that have fallen to the ground,
In which this large tree was once dressed.

See how the branches are torn and wilted,
The weight bearing down too heavy to hold,
The heart of this tree looks worn and jilted,
Were once, it grew young and bold.

The life this tree in the past supported,
Has shrivelled and given up the ghost,
Life is suddenly not worth living,
Without the will and energy of its host.

The birds have flown the coop,
Aware that the tree is prematurely dying,
The lizards and insects have shifted house,
They don't want to hear the tree groaning and sighing.

Now, take your chainsaw in hand,
And put this tree out of its misery,
As it no longer has the will to strive,

Please ensure that the cut is quick and clean,
It would be horrific for the tree to survive.

Now, put your chainsaw down,
And survey the scene,
Feel the air filled with sorrow and pain,
Notice our love in amongst the carnage,
As this tree and our love are the same!

Forty Years
A Miracle Today

I spotted something today,
That almost made me cry,
She was sixty-three,
And he was seventy-five.

He was lying in a hospital bed,
She refused to leave his side,
He was her husband,
She was his bride.

Forty years we've been married,
That's what I heard them say,
I wonder if they know how lucky they are,
As that's a miracle today.

I couldn't take my eyes off them,
They were in a world of their own,
Only there for each other,
In their own personal zone.

But you know what really surprised me,
The love that shone in their eyes,
After all those forty years,
Their love had never died.

The Power of Love
The Emotions, the Feelings, the Fullness of Heart

She softly runs her finger down the back of his arm,
Smiling as his tiny hairs stood on end, liking it to a thousand
caterpillar legs,
She holds her breath as he gently stirs, a moan escaping his
parted lips,
As he rises from the deepest slumber, his sigh is one that
quietly begs.

She moves closer to his naked back, slow kisses mingling
down his spine,
Watching as his eyelids flutter in intensity, the purest groan
drew deep,
He moves, rubbing against her swollen breasts, nipples erect,
No longer trying to hold onto his dreams, his distance sleep.

She leans over and whispers into his ear,
Smiling as, she croons, *"Wake up honey, let's celebrate,*
It's a new day, full of our dawning love,
Cementing our bond, our fire, our forever fate."

He rolls onto his back, eyes full of want and desire,
Who needs sleep when brandishing by the side of this

beautiful girl?
Her gentleness, her pureness, her love, her dreams,
She so unselfishly shares with him as their love unfurls.

He runs his hands through the silken waterfall of her hair,
Playfully flicking her bangs from her forehead to free a space
for his loving kiss,
She sighs deeply at the connection, in awe of her brewing
emotions,
As he whispers his love, giving her the memories, she'll later
reminisce.

Her heart fills with the sheer beauty of their joy,
As they lose themselves to instinct, to welcoming release,
While they love and laugh, flirt and kiss,
Becoming more frenzied until they sink back to earth in
peace.

She lays her head on his chest, her adoring eyes searching his
face,
As he lovingly smiles, his happiness at being the one she
chose,
He knows she's one in a million; he caught the luck of the
draw,
Plucked from the bouquet the prettiest of rose.

He smiles as he loses himself in the fantasy of their future,
Knowing he'll fight to keep this woman within the safety of
his arms,
Defending her honour, her desires, her wishes and satisfying
her deepest of needs,

Destroying all in the vicinity who attempt to damage or harms.

This woman doesn't realise her own beauty, her pureness of heart,
But he knows she deserves to be worshipped and full of desire,
He'll see that she wreathes in ecstasy and bliss,
As he loves her gently, knowing she'll forever be his to pleasure and admire.

Living on Tenterhooks
How Has This Become Her Life

She stops to listen as she hears the key slot into the front
door,
Hands wet as she pauses with a dish in her hand,
Listening carefully, trying to determine his mood,
Did he have a good day, or did it not go to plan?

Her heart beats faster as she hears the squeal of the door
hinges,
She turns to face the doorway, listening to his tread,
Are they stamping down the hallway? Or softly trodden?
She waits on tenterhooks; this time of the day, one she's
learned to dread.

Her breath catches in her throat as he steadily nears,
And as he rounds the corner, she wears a tentative smile,
Waiting, anticipating, nervously anxious,
As her stomach's acid rises and, she tastes her own bile.

She expels a gasp of relief as she sees his face for the first
time,
He looks relaxed; a large grin stretches across his lips,
She hurries to the refrigerator and grabs a cold can of beer,
Smiling graciously as she hands it to him and he thankfully

takes a sip.

But then suddenly, the can is sailing across the length of the
room,
Beer swirling upon the walls, the floor and dripping from her
hair,
He slaps her across the cheek with an open-palmed hand,
And she falls to the floor, curls into a ball and gasps for air.

She sobs as a foot lands across her aching ribs,
Hearing a bone crack, not a first for her at all,
She sobs quietly in desperation, knowing this could go on for
hours,
As she attempts to draw herself in and make herself small.

He begins to yell and scream about her uselessness,
How she can never do anything right,
Each roar backed up with a carefully placed punch,
While she cowers away from him in fright.

She can now smell the alcohol on his breath,
The stench of the last few hours drowning his sorrow,
She lays still, praying, sobbing, waiting,
Wishing for today to end quickly and a better tomorrow.

Wallowing in the Forgotten Feelings Buried Deep within My Heart

As I close my eyes and delve into the deepest chambers of
my heart,
I find you nestled there so lovingly, mine forever,
We no longer meet on the physical plane,
But our love was the best, those heartstrings we'll never
sever.

I live for the memories, the feelings as we once knew,
The preciousness of your every touch,
The whispers of sweet nothings that made me smile,
Missed—yes, so terribly much.

The gifts bestowed by a loving thought, a kind message,
Each line the library shelves of my most secret heart space,
Pulled down and inspected on a regular basis,
So, I'll never forget our love, your memories, your never-
ending grace.

There were so many firsts that were ours,
Words were not needed; your touch was my all,
Communication over long distances a breeze,
Your support, your assistance, your shoulder; all mine
whenever I'd call.

Tomorrows, taken for granted,
Our loss,
But that doesn't mean I'll ever regret it,
We—yes, we were worth that expensive cost.

There were so many moments in which we were blessed,
Moments that were golden and exquisite to life, even just one time,
Many people are never so lucky as to experience even once,
But we had many; we were given a gift the day you became mine.

I can still feel your gaze lovingly falling upon my face,
The desire that burned deep within your eyes,
The goosebumps your words cascaded against my skin,
The music to my ears when I'd hear your breathless sighs.

I'm not sure I ever did thank you for your time, your peace, your storms,
Never realising the golden casket that we held within our hearts,
That's not to say they weren't real; they weren't the magic in our stars,
For they were exactly what we needed when it all fell apart.

The hours, the music, the love, the sensations, the breathless minutes,
Live in that bloody chamber, locked tightly from the others who visit,
The walls are lined with your words, your gazes, your silence,

The memories golden, precious, so delightfully exquisite.

In that chamber, you'll always be mine,
And forever and a day, I'll always be yours,
Our room, our memories, our love, our lessons, our destiny,
Bound for you only; to the rest, they find locked doors.

I wallow in the souvenirs that line the walls,
I bathe in the words that hang in the air,
I shower in the feelings that saturate like raindrops,
And I promise you my love, my loyalty, my care.

Love Lasts Longer
Laughter Lifts Lowness

Love, longing, like, lust, loss,
Literally, life lived,
Long live love, long live life,
Let's learn love's lovely languages.

Less lamenting losses,
Letting laughter lighten life,
Like last laughs, laugh louder,
Live longer, live leisurely.

Listen lovingly, learning life's lessons,
Let lopsided lewdness lose,
Leaking lies less likely,
Love lives longer, luckily.

Loneliness leaves longing laments,
Lasting lengthy limits,
Lyrical language luxurious lessening,
Letting life linger lovingly.

Lumping lover's leftovers,
Least lying lightens loads lingering,
Lastly, life lays loose lessons,

Letting learning liken lower.

Lust, lost love, lessening laughter,
Less life, less light,
Let loose, lighten lacerations,
Leniency, let's love lighten life.

Liken limiting loftiness,
Longing less likely lynched,
Love likewise lulls lugubriously,
Lifting low levels lastingly.

Let love linger,
Learn loss lessens,
Laugh louder,
Lively living longingly, lasting lovingly.

Fire and Ice
Their Love Is Both Extremes

She remembers the night with a smile,
A glorious night of love, passion and fire,
A single touch sends shivers down her spine,
The beginning of their love, their building desire.

She lays and relives the moments of the night,
The feelings, the sensations, the ultimate bliss,
Her smile widens as she reignites her wanting,
Leaning over as, she wakes him with a kiss.

A slow grin works its way across his sensuous lips,
As he pretends to stay still within his slumber,
But she knows he has awoken,
And he knows she's got his number.

They revisit the passion that has been building,
Smiles and moans the order of the morning,
Their bodies slick with sweat,
As the lightening hours of the sun a-dawning.

The kids are chattering outside their door,
As they climb from their lover's bed,
The day begins, their duty calls,

As the chaos of living quells their fire instead.

The noise increases into a crescendo,
As the day begins in a rush,
An argument builds as the panic mounts,
The silent screams in her head calling hush-hush.

The crushing pressure takes its toll,
He begins to yell and scream at her sacrifice,
They battle with words to and fro,
As their passion turns to ice.

Finally, the kids are dropped off at school,
And he is dressed, ready to head to work,
The noise has dissipated to a stony silence,
Neither acknowledging the pain nor hurt.

Just another day in their life of responsibilities,
Another round of commitment and assurance,
And as the day draws to a close once more,
They laugh away the conflict, marvelling at their endurance.

He apologises for the morning turmoil,
She accepts it with her grace,
As they climb into bed that evening,
And allow their passion to take its place.

The nights are heated, made for love,
Their passion on fire, their love celebrated,
The days are cooler, built on bricks of ice,
Pressurised and aggravated.

A Destined Love
A Fateful Meeting One Fine Day

He sits staring into space, daydreaming,
Thinking of his plans for that very night,
A date with destiny, he feels it in his veins,
A dinner, a relaxing wine, a night to excite.

It all started a couple of weeks ago,
Wandering along the boardwalk, stopping dead,
There is a vision, an incredible goddess,
Wandering along in leisure just up ahead.

His paces speed up considerably,
As he follows in her trail,
He needs a closer look, a need more important than
breathing,
Adamant, he had to inspect her every fine detail.

As he swaggers up alongside this glorious vision,
He realises she must be a muse from another world,
Perfection, astonishing beauty, a glimmer of paradise,
He's lost his ability to speak, shocked at the sight of this
wonderful girl.

He opens his mouth to stutter, abhorrent at his tongue-

tiredness,
A cough, a splutter and finally, a whistle under his breath,
This man has fallen under her spell, a classic case of love at
first sight,
He realises he is hers from this moment until his death.

She glances across at him in amusement,
Perfectly aware of the effect she has cast upon him,
She smiles gracefully, leaving him weak in the knees,
And when he asks her shyly if she'll do dinner, she says yes
on a whim.

That precocious fateful meeting,
Was a destiny of awakening, an epic life-changing,
As they both fell into the deepening of their relationship,
Sure, it was a fateful arranging.

He sits and daydreams,
Wondering how it all came to be,
This blessing in the guise of a goddess,
Unlocking his heart and setting his love free.

My Heart's Song
Thank You to My Band and Chorus Members

A new year has arrived and with it, my gratitude,
Today, my heart is full, beating to my favourite song,
Every tune, every heartbeat, is a pulsing haven,
Where I'm grateful for those in my life, where they belong.

I have family that are nestled in safely,
Sitting in the corners, anchored in tight,
They beat their drum in the rhythm of love,
A large part of my band as is their birthright.

Playing the harmonies, their voices loud,
Are the friends that I treasure evermore,
Long-term people who've hung in through my sour notes,
And freshly made friends who I just adore.

There's very little room left in my heart,
As I'm blessed with those who're the absolute best,
Some hit the high notes, others the low bass,
Musical perfection, every nuance expressed.

I thought about cutting a record,
But unless you're part of the group, you'd not understand,

The music, the notes, the words, the dance,
Of my one-of-a-kind rock 'n' roll band.

What you'd hear is a song terribly out of tune,
The clash of the drums overriding the blues,
The guitar rift racing faster as it heads to the heavens,
To include the band members who've paid their dues.

The bass will be loud, thumping to my heart's song,
The vocals rise and fall on my deepest breaths,
The harmonica, oh, that harmonica
Weaving its way through with sorrows and deaths.

But on those glorious days like today,
When we are all in tune, happiness spreads,
The love in my heart, the gratitude for you all,
Sweeps through the universe in my musical threads.

Unearthing the Precious Memories
Of the Glorious Love Once Held

Wandering the valleys of her mind, reminiscing
Over obstacles, periods of hardship and sorrow,
Looking under crevices, inside darkened caves,
Witnessing the days of yesteryear and not those of
tomorrow.

She often walks the dusty halls of her archives,
In search of the wonderful lessons she has learned,
Those of bittersweet words and lingering touches,
To those, she wallowed in pity when horribly burned.

She climbs the vines of forgetfulness,
Scrounging through the dumped trash of past rejection,
She scuffles through the age-old memories,
Until she uncovers one of such sheer perfection.

There, she visits for a while,
Remembering,
The wonderful minutes of all she experienced,
And those feelings that left her trembling.

The nights of passionate love,
The sharing of her past with that one so dear,

Surrendering into open arms of comfort,
Trusting he'll deliver from her worst fear.

The early morning conversations,
Whispered into ears of silent understanding
Of long-lost dreams, goals and wishes,
As he loves her with his entire heart, fulfilled and undemanding.

The pride he wore upon his face,
When introducing her to his life,
His family, his friends,
His commitment as he made her his wife.

The shoulder he gave her to lean on,
His strength hers to use at will,
Loving and learning her every need,
His world offered in humbleness to fulfil.

Her very wish is his to command,
As he worships the ground beneath her feet,
His thoughts never far from her wisdom,
Knowing she made him feel complete.

All this she stumbles upon while searching
In the deepest, darkest of crevices and cracks,
Until she unearths the greatest memory of all,
Studying her find, measuring the parallax.

She once struck gold within this moment,
And tried to hold on tight,

But the good times slipped through her fingers,
As their love gave up the fight.

Now, she's left with these golden memories,
Ones that hurt, so she buried them deep,
But now enough time has bypassed the ending,
And she's unearthing the precious memories she wishes to
keep.

The Bitter Truth
Learned the Hard Way

A day dawned in unwelcoming light,
A heart has broken, torn to shreds,
A night of sheer agony best forgotten,
The sun shadowing her fear and dread.

She was forewarned,
Yes, that is true,
But she needed to learn,
To see it all through.

A tear rolls down her hot pink cheeks,
As she digests the lesson unfolding,
Her thoughts a shambles, unthinkable,
Her feelings trodden, her love withholding.

Embarrassed, yes, to say the least,
Hurting, of course, it's how she learns,
The plan crumbles,
While her dreams and wishes horribly burns.

She reaches with a forgotten hand,
Begging for the bitter truth as it is told,
Wanting the honesty regardless of the pain,

Each word heard while fiercely controlled.

The sound of the unheard scolding,
Bashes around her in tornado gusts,
She curls in upon her horror,
Knowing she'll accept it, she truly must.

Believing she was finished, an unsavoury end,
The start of the loss and the beginning of a new,
Wandering the days of solitude and loneliness,
Appreciating the sordid state of blue.

Day after day, regret at the forefront,
Wishing for it to be different, nothing more than a bad
dream,
Sleepless nights, tears a sodden,
Painful memories and a silent scream.

But unbeknownst to her in her sorrow,
Tomorrow dawns a bright new day,
The sun does shine golden upon her spirit,
As it squanders the dark shadows forever away.

Her face delights with the brightest smile,
Discovering the loss was exactly as it should be,
Simplifying her life, letting it shine,
Unchaining her heart and setting her free.

The way forward is coated in glitter,
Stardust and moonbeams surround her soul,
She's where she needs to be in all her glory,

The best version of her yet, her magnificence whole.

She realises the pain was a necessary lesson,
A temporary patch of defeat,
Allowing her future to shine with belief,
As she wakes to a new day, feeling majestically complete.

A False Declaration
A Living Lie

She waited patiently for your return,
Not knowing there was little chance,
You'd made up your mind, did what was best for you,
The last thing on your mind was an old romance.

You saunter through your day nursing your ego,
Not a thought given to the love you left behind,
She pines as she silently longs to see your face,
But you've no sympathy for her pain of any kind.

She believed your spoken promises,
You convinced her with your repeated dribble,
She felt your love, your care, your lies,
Silent throughout your anger, she'd never quibble.

Her heart beat in hope and dreams,
Seeing you for someone you could never be,
Your true colours began to shine,
But as they say, love is too blind to see.

She mourns your absence,
Do you think of her as you go about your day?
Imagining the devastation she is currently surviving,

As she learns of the cruelty in which you play?

She sobs herself to sleep in the darkening hours,
Blaming herself for the fault of her aching heart,
Struggling through the hours of your betrayal,
Not understanding your need to part.

Once conquered, you move on to the next,
The hunt is the prize you desire,
The captured heart tossed aside,
Another notch on your belt for you to acquire.

She'll eventually count her blessings,
As she realises, she had a lucky escape,
Your love was not healthy; no, it's extremely toxic,
A war zone, a destructive landscape.

Her heart may be scarred from the sheer battle,
Fought alone as she traversed your battleground,
But the lessons she gained through the pain,
Freed her for the abundant self-love she found.

She has now become terribly guarded,
Protective of her sacred heart,
Love has left her weary,
Teaching her to think and live smart.

She'll not give up on love,
As you've taught her well, the destruction
Of a false declaration, an ego's promise,
Not of love but instead a conquered seduction.

First Glance
And Their Love Story Begins

Sunshine on a dark, cloudy day,
Wisps of happiness adorn the very air,
In which she inhales,
Daydreams star in her eyes,
A single meeting of the heart so rare.

Dreaming of the potential possibilities,
As her heart skips a beat or two,
Joy eclipses the rising sun,
As she remembers the glorious night,
When his aura surrounded her through and through.

The whispered gasps of ecstasy,
As the song of his voice pierced her ears,
Harmonies floating between his words,
Meant for her, heard by no others,
As her hazy thought clears.

Like smoke on the waters,
His eyes capture the beauty of her dreams,
Reeling across her face in blatant honesty,
Starstruck by the intensity between the pair,
Captured perfectly, it seems.

Winters have been long,
As they both patiently waited,
Single in their solitude,
Breath held,
Twins within their agony, frustrated.

Standing solo within their future plans,
Until that gaze, they cast upon the other,
Knowing destiny has intertwined,
Working its magic,
Cruising their negativity to smother.

Their silent promises are now broken,
The chains upon their hearts now shattered,
The undeniable connection hard hit,
At just a single glance,
The rest of the world no longer mattered.

A shy smile graces her plump red lips,
A downward cast of her shining eyes,
He smiles inwardly, knowing she is now his,
As he crosses the room to stand by her side,
She quickly glances up and heaves heavenly sighs.

Her heart skips another beat,
At the touch of his fingers upon her chin,
She raises her head to adventure into his gaze,
Testing the waters to ascertain,
If she should allow her love for him to begin.

He laughs at her thoughts,
Really, she has no choice,
Fate has stepped in and taken the reins of their love,
They belong to one another now,
As romance has finally found its voice.

A chance meeting,
Many would argue not,
A relationship of certainty,
One destined from the fateful day of birth,
A day Cupids' arrow was surely shot.

The future is theirs,
To guard at will,
No longer solo but two hearts forever entwined,
Serendipity at play,
As the vessel of their love does overfill.

Fingers knotted in future years,
Unlimited possibilities theirs to hold,
Paradise theirs to mould,
Into a strength, a blossom of love,
A famous promise untold!

The Release of His Pain
Life Is Short, but This Was Bigger

The weekend is here, it's Friday night,
As he walks into his local watering hole,
Determined to drink himself stupid,
Because of his broken heart, she stole.

"*A beer if you'll please,*" he requests of the bartender,
"*Keep them coming, one or two just won't do,*"
As he tips his glass to his friends and throws it back,
We can see it's going to be a big night, with a lot more than
a few.

His heart is bleeding on his sleeve,
Torn and shredded by that girl he loved deeply,
She tossed it aside without a care or a backward glance,
Loudly, mind you, she certainly didn't break his heart
discreetly.

He tosses the second beer down,
Realising it's not got what it takes,
"*Bartender, drop the hard liquor if you will,*
This beer's not going to fill the cracks and breaks."

As the whiskey is poured, he yells,

"Skip the rocks if you don't mind, I'll take it neat,"
First glass burns on its way down,
But his heart is in so much pain he can't feel the heat.

As you can imagine, he was a dribbling mess after a few hours,
We had to see him home that night,
Tossing him on top of his bed as his tears flowed,
He was left with no more fight.

We tried to tell him that life is too short,
But this girl has really bought him to his knees,
For weeks, he stumbled through this thing called life,
Nursing his heartbreaking mental disease.

He soon discovered no amount of alcohol would do the trick,
As his pain and torment was bigger than it all,
No escape, suffering day after day,
He never stumbled and tripped; no, she'd made him fall.

This was bigger than he could handle,
As he welcomed the end of his darkness, his brood,
No goodbyes, no excuses,
This was bigger than him, a larger magnitude.

We buried him under his favourite shady tree,
Knowing he was now at peace,
Although he couldn't comprehend the pain it caused us,
He was laid to rest, his pain and suffering now released.

The Release of Her Pain
Life Is Short, but This Was Bigger

She'd only just heard the news,
The terrible words cut her like a blade,
She knew she was to blame,
Oh, the terrible price he paid.

She never dreamed that it'd result in his passing,
The sordid price of her darkness,
Her destructiveness,
Her callousness, her cruelty in all its starkness.

She never meant to hurt him,
But she was in a bad place at the time,
Now, he's paid the ultimate price,
Oh, it's her bloody crime.

She lifted her glass to her lips,
Endeavouring to stop the constant pain,
The guilt, the horror and her never-ending shame,
A mark on her heart, a rotten stain.

The whiskey is not doing as she needs,
His memory is imprinted on her agonising mind,
She'll never find forgiveness,

Nor is she deserving; she wasn't at all kind.

She lays back against her pillow,
Holding his picture in front of her face,
As she raises her other hand to her temple,
Pulling the trigger in disgrace.

We buried her under the same tree,
Together, they now rest in peace,
We hope she finds her forgiveness,
And her pain is now released.

Her Magnificent Self
Born from the Ashes of Toxic Love

She worshipped the ground on which you walked,
Even while it was she you trampled,
Adoring your every move, your every word,
Your dreams, your wishes and the love she sampled.

And yet you broke her very soul,
Destroyed her with your so-called love and desire,
Stripped her bare to her very core,
Setting her veins of love on fire.

She revelled in your every happiness,
Bending over backwards to light up your day,
Smiling broadly at any attention you throw her way,
Listening to every word of love you say.

Until that is, you tossed her like she was trash,
Your footsteps imprinted upon her forehead in bloody
tattoos,
As you stormed out of the bounds of honesty,
Leaving her in a puddle of sobs and blues.

She shouldered your treatment with heavy sighs,
Tolerating the abuse that you called adoration,

The light in her eyes slowly dulling,
Until her love is left in a pile of cremation.

Was that your original intention?
To break the back of her beauty and innocence?
To leave her a tangled web of sorrow and pain?
To cull her sheer magnificence?

But as you didn't stick around the kill site,
You didn't bear witness to her incredible strength,
As she rose from the ashes, a brilliant flaming phoenix,
Rebuilding her esteem, her worth, every harrowing length.

Now, when the sun rises on another precious day,
She opens her eyes and sends thanks your way,
Grateful for the power and strength you helped her find,
To become the perfect womanly spirit she places on display.

Pride Has No Place
Not in Any Loving Relationship

The time cannot be returned,
The missed opportunities guised as rejection,
The most expensive commodity is the hours on any given
day,
Consider the consequences of withholding your affection.

Love is destroyed by the shallowness and coldness,
Of stupidity and pig-headedness,
What changed?
Know that your actions leave a loved one's emotions a mess.

Is it worth the loss of love?
The pain you cause by no longer being considerate
Of another's feelings, the hurt you drive,
Especially when the actions are deliberate.

Don't spout the words of love.
After your narcissistic ways,
Proving your actions speak louder than words,
Leaving pain that lasts for days.

Why?
They're left wondering without an answer.

After years of closeness, loyalty and happiness,
Love is eroded by a fast-acting cancer.

Please reconsider, make a last-ditch effort,
Bring the universe back onto an even keel,
You're close to losing their love forever,
And the regret will be horrendous, not how you'll want to feel.

Pride is an expense you cannot afford,
Life is short and you've no idea of the time left,
Don't stand at their graveside in disarray,
And realise the horror of your actions became time's theft.

Tomorrow could be too late,
Neither of you are invincible,
A blink of an eye is all it takes,
Think deeply before the power of loss becomes convincible.

Love is forgiveness,
Accepting that no one is perfect,
There's no room for revenge,
Stop now before your love is irreparably wrecked.

Be the bigger person,
Hold your loved one near,
Let the water under the bridge dissipate,
And don't hold onto stupidity because of fear.

The Language of Love
The Sweetest Language That Should Rule Our World

Words are not the most powerful language,
No, it is the power of love that sustains us all,
The language that whispers directly to our soul,
The magic of love is one that sends us all its call.

Silence coveted within the walls of someone's love,
Is the golden bliss experienced in all its glory,
The shower of intentions moulded with joy,
Whispering directly to your heart its powerful story.

Words spoken within the boundaries of love,
Are softly harmonising the waves of its spell,
Weaving and ducking through your bloodstream,
Guiding and highlighting the love it does tell.

Washing over every loving relationship,
Basking in the sunlight in which it dawns your day,
Even the gentlest scolding done with love,
Is a lesson learned and not a harsh word to say.

The fingertips of desire whisper across your skin,
Blooming a rose of such sheer perfection,

Hormones respond deliciously, aspiring,
With no hesitation of returned affection.

Tomorrow, the darkness will disappear a while,
As giggles and laughter lovingly grace each trail,
The heart at its fullest and all is right with the world,
The strong grow stronger and love supports the frail.

Every decision made in the honour of love,
Moves us forward on our given trek,
The winding roads of our future glisten,
Until the peaceful dying of hatred is checked.

Wonderful thoughts change our perceptions,
When the flow of love is at its pinnacle,
Surrounded by feelings of bliss and happiness,
Outcomes even the most disbelieving and cynical.

Strive for a lifetime of love and harmony,
Blessings and miracles a sure bet,
Learn the power of conversing with love,
And feel the positivity as your future is set.

Each day brings unfathomable possibilities,
To honour the hours and minutes freely given,
Perfection is not the absence of mistakes,
But in the generosity of love, forgiving.

Smile through the pain of losing love,
Knowing it was not given sincerely,
Believe in the day that'll arrive unexpectedly,

When the power of love is honoured clearly.

Wallow in the clouds of desire and wishes,
Harmoniously attracting a never-ending shower of adoration,
Live your life within the universal power of devotion,
As you open your heart to love's exploration.

If all is done in the name of true love,
Less destruction will ensue throughout our day,
Life will be smoother, the pain more tolerant,
And we'll be loyal within our faith that all is okay.

To Be Horribly Human
The Emotions Rule

The eyes open, the heart beats, the excitement begins,
A new day, a new relationship, a new friend,
The giddiness of it all, the smile that graces a face,
Confidence, hope for the future, anticipation, the love to transcend.

A few hours of company, fun and adventure,
The heart is a little lighter, problems pushed aside,
The deliciousness and newness of a connection,
The emotional upheaval of a new possibility, two beings collide.

The happiness of compatibility, the strength of dreams,
The initial expectations, the pictured future in one's head,
At first, all is swell, going as planned, ecstatically simple,
An unrealistic dream, but real-life intercepts instead.

Another day is dawning, eyes open in trepidation,
Anxiety causes the heart to race, over-thinking at play,
Questions unanswered doubts steadily creep within,
Worry and concern at the forefront of everything they say.

Communication has broken, unhappy thoughts ignored,

The barrier between two people heightens,
If only a word or two was spoken, discussed honestly,
But within the delicate balance of a relationship, one it frightens.

The ending is on the horizon; no longer fighting for a stay of execution,
The inevitability has been taken on board, accepted,
The future dreams are forgotten, wasted,
All due to the reality of possibly being rejected.

The complexity of human nature,
The sadness of being horribly human, imperfectly flawed,
The relationship could have been saved, certainly salvaged,
If with honesty and trust, the emotions were explored.

Unfortunately, those things that make us horribly human,
Especially the complexity of past experiences and emotions
Ruin and destroy such wonderful relationships, love lost,
If we don't communicate, fearing the up and down motions.

We hold our own expectations, our own needs and heart-rendering triggers,
Projecting these onto those we absolutely adore,
Fighting our own demons, insecurities and heartbreaks,
Blaming the other for our pain, fears, terror and more.

Love Is Not Easy.
But with the Right Person, It Can
Be Worth It

Your scent sails across the westerly winds,
Bringing a smile to her sweet, glorious face,
Hard work, male desire, nature's essence,
Spellbind her within paper and lace.

She waits with bated breath,
Knowing you are hers and hers alone,
Date night, an edge of excitement,
Ending in the most precious erotic zone.

Two people destined to meet,
Hearts beating in perfect tune,
Love at first sight, maybe,
Starstruck under the light of a blue moon.

Ecstasy flows within her veins,
Fingertips breathing in the scent of your skin,
A golden touch, a sensitive brush of her hair,
Goosebumps raised from neck to shin.

Welcoming sensuality like never before known,
Breathing her very essence deep within your adoration,

Savouring, learning her deepest secrets,
As every inch is given freely for your exploration.

Sunlight dances through the strands of her hair,
Plump pink lips pouting in sheer perfection,
A come-hither glance is thrown your way,
Her needs and wishes cast in your direction.

Bathing in your attention,
Her glorious nakedness with goddess ability,
She moans in pleasure with every passing grace,
As she crests the waves into peaceful tranquillity.

Her eyes fill with desire as they lock onto yours,
A graceful smile winds across her lips,
She rolls into the crest of your strong arms,
Purring prettily into sleep, she slips.

You watch in wonder at this stunning princess,
One with whom you traverse the years to come,
Your love grows daily,
As your pain for the past has finally succumb.

You lay there and follow your pending dreams,
As they wander your mind, open to all possibilities,
Love has changed you from the inside out,
Freeing you from the trauma and past hostilities.

You owe it all to this woman who lays by your side,
And she owes you for her recent dive into paradise,
You both need to protect the gift you've been blessed with,

And be prepared for each battle wills and painful sacrifice.

Love doesn't come easy,
But can extend to perfection,
If coaxed and drawn out with infinite patience,
Attention to detail and loads of affection.

Leave tomorrow in the future to take care of itself,
As you both muster the courage to traverse through today,
Extend your morals to include passion and loyalty,
And you'll find your love's cost is easy to pay.

Never lay your head down on the back of an argument,
Wisdom holds out for those who talk it out,
Allow love to gentle your anger,
And ensure you stay calm, never abuse and shout.

The effort you both expend will come back tenfold,
The years will vanish in the blink of an eye,
But the joy you'll both experience with a little hard work,
Will see that your love excels never to die.

The Smell of Love
Sensational Scents

The aroma of a single red rose,
Received on her very first date,
Pressed in between the pages of her favourite book,
The scent escapes into the air as she opens the page to
liberate.

The heated leather molecules captured in his car,
As he drives her to the lookout on a starry night,
The scent moulding around their bodies,
As they make out in the backseat in pure delight.

The scented bubble bath bathing her skin,
She luxuriates before dressing just for him,
As he escorts her to a dazzling ball,
Dancing within a cloud of her perfume, in which she swims.

The glorious fragrance of a field of wildflowers,
As he bends his knee and asks for her hand,
The warming smell of her wedding bouquet,
As she waltzes the aisle to make him her man.

The faint aroma of his empty pillow,
Laying beside her, smothering her in all his glory,

Reminders of his peaceful face,
As he slumbers beside her as part of her story.

The aroma of her first home-cooked meal,
As he walks in the door from a hard day's work,
She hands him a fragrant glass of ale,
And dances past him in an alluring mini-skirt.

The innocent smell of their love child's freshly bathed hair,
The epic atoms of love's perfect blessing,
As his mini-me now calls her mum,
The very definition of love expressing.

The faintest of scents in his greying hair,
As he holds her aged body close to his side,
She lifts her lips for a last kiss goodbye,
And smiles as she leaves this world; she quietly died.

Now, he wanders his final years all alone,
With only his favourite scents to lessen his grief,
The forgotten rose pressed in between the pages,
Of whose scent reminds him of his greatest love,
Allowing him to live out his last years in loving relief.

No Rescue from Tomorrow
Alone with Her Heartbreak

I watch as she lifts her glass to her lips, closing her eyes,
As she tastes the sublime icy cold liquor that races down her throat,
She opens her eyes and feels my gaze upon her beauty,
Turning her head, giving me a sad nod, her eyes terribly remote.

She turns back to the bar to saviour her drink,
Lost in her brokenness, her sad thoughts,
I guarantee she's here to escape her man and his treatment,
His cruelty is what would have seen this melancholy wrought.

I feel her sorrow, her pain, from across the room,
Deciding to approach her and offer her some solace,
She shakes her head at me as I take the stool by her side,
But I ignore this head shake and take my place.

"I'm not another guy trying to pick you up,"
I explain as I sit,
"I can see your pain and let me guess, it's caused by a man,"
"You'd guess right," she spit.

"I saw you sitting, staring at your drink, waiting for your ice to melt,"
I say, *"And please let me tell you, you don't need that guy,"*
I silently wait to see how she'd react to that,
But instead, she breathes deep and lets out an agonising sigh.

She looks me in the eye, smiling a little wider,
And to my surprise, she introduces herself to me,
Telling me that I got it dead right,
And she's planning on setting him free.

As the night wears on, the drinks too many to count,
Her smile grows wider, her words happier; he's been forgotten,
However, in the back of her eyes, I can still see the sorrow,
But for these few hours, I helped her not to feel so rotten.

We both know it's a temporary respite,
She'll feel the heartbreak fully tomorrow,
And she'll be alone, no guy sitting on the other side of the room,
Worried about her mood, her pain and her sorrow.

The Heartbeat of the Enchanted
The Ultimate Feeling to Fill the Heart

The heart is both a twofold blessing and a heart-wrenching
nemesis,
Holding our memories of love and woes,
The best of the best, the worst of the worst,
Memories of friends and others of foes.

The pain shatters and often breaks us,
Until love comes along to help us heal,
The ups and downs, the brokenness and new,
Without this vessel, we'd never know how we feel.

Memories of yesterday and yesteryear,
Make us into the gifts that we are,
The love we fill our hearts with,
The feelings that become our guiding star.

The pain a lesson of which to learn,
The betrayals of our family and past friends,
Causing the deepest of scorching heartbreak,
That only loving memories are the reason it ends.

Guard this precious vessel with the strength of your soul,

Don't let those that have betrayed you back in,
Treasure the beauty of those that connect with love,
As it is these gifts that will see you win.

Feel the good and the bad of love's past messages,
Learn the lessons of your unique heart,
Know that love is the ultimate fulfilment,
So, say goodbye to those that need to part.

Don't look back at the losses in regret,
Those losses were not love in its purity,
But the sadness of those that caused the pain,
Those feelings of jealousy and insecurity.

Remember the joy of a heart full of love,
Strive for this perfection on a daily basis,
Travel the rainbows of caring and empathy
On the way to life's loving oasis.

We needed the pain to learn the joy,
Without it, we'd take it all for granted,
But don't wallow in the sorrow,
Instead, live in the heartbeat of the enchanted.

The Future Was Always Ours
I've No Doubt Whatsoever

The memories stick in my mind; the years haven't aged them,
I remember your silken touch as your fingertips breezed over my skin,
The subtle kisses running down my spine, sweetening the sensation,
Your tenderness was my ultimate bliss, our own personal lead-in.

I dream of us nightly, fantasies held from when we were our best,
The sunny days, the widest grins, the pleasure, the pain I miss,
I reminisce often of the sound of your voice, the touch of your breath,
The softness of your long blonde hair, the enchantment of your kiss.

Remember, we dreamed of forever; the future was always ours,
The years we'd planned out, the travels, the children, the desires,
I still hold these tightly locked within my heart, yours

forevermore,
Because a love like ours, the deepest connection, that love
never expires.

I hold the knowledge within my soul, knowing deeply we
will be again,
Maybe not quite tomorrow, but definitely soon, essentially
more,
Another daybreak spent within the security of your arms,
Better, stronger, powerfully tethered in the heart of the one I
adore.

Destiny runs within our veins, moulding the essence of two
hearts,
The daily beating of our pulse, the music to which we dance,
The distance diminishes with every minute; our time is near,
As we wander the path of our definitive second chance.

I await with bated breath for the magical starry night,
Ripe with anticipation, eagerness intense,
Our first glance will be all-encompassing,
The universal signal allowing our relationship to
recommence.

One Precious Second Opened My Eyes, My Heart, My World

A connection to my soul with just one glance into your eyes,
As I walked past you in the grocery aisle,
A heartbeat in time, a fleeting moment,
One that opened my world in a short period of time.

The connection was strong,
Just a minute in amongst my lifetime of hours,
But it opened my heart, changed my day,
Left an indelible memory for years to come.

Seconds was all it took to open my eyes to a different world,
To change my perception of the love of mankind,
Hit by a tsunami of long-forgotten feelings
That I'd buried within my yesterdays.

My breath stutters from my mouth,
My feet stand still, forgetting how to move,
Frozen in the space of the universe,
Stumbling, falling, finding love of another,
In a spasm of a second,
Every cell of mine expanded, changed, swelled.

All it took was a glance from a complete stranger!

An innocent grocery shopping trip,
Blew my world to smithereens,
A beating from the other world, a bashing, a reminder,
Of a life as it could be.

We never crossed paths again after that unreal day,
But the lesson imparted from one fleeting moment,
Defined my life from that perfect second,
And helped make me into the person I am today.

The impact was monumental in ways you'll never know,
So, I send thanks to that one human whom I cannot even
name,
My world stood on its head for that precious second,
Showering me in a stranger's love and empathy,
Opening my heart,
And connecting with my soul.

A Wild Dependability
The Final Testing of the Waters

The cracks begin to show when the pain escalates,
A heart broken, bloody and bruised,
Tormented with love's rocky abrasions,
Tearing open unsealed scarring,
Ripped raw and shredded to tatters.

Once locked and loaded with revenge,
Softens on meeting a single-minded connection,
Doubt and insecurities abound; we question,
The suitability of testing the waters once again,
Striving for forgiveness and healing.

Hope is a powerful incentive,
Dreams unlock the coded heartbeats at will,
The rhythm chants upon our breath,
Releasing the pain, the past torture, the fake memories,
Until resistance is once more overcome.

Silence of adoration overpowers our hesitation,
Bonding the rapid butterflies fluttering within,
Excitement building within the future possibilities,
Smothering the trepidation, the anxious, the reversing
temptation,
Opening the heart, the mind, the body to love once again.

Systematically proving the best is yet to come,
Swallowing your pride and stubborn refusals,
Believing in the infinity of externalisation,
Growing together over the familiarity of the years,
To become the one connection that holds on.

The pain of lost love nothing more than a valuable lesson,
Of inconsistencies unwelcome within a loving heart,
The pounding of terror, not a home to settle for,
But the gentle flutter of butterfly wings,
The ultimate beginning of something reborn.

Welcome the blessing with gratitude,
But don't strangle the freedom of emotions,
Flow with the loving imperfections,
Capturing the idiosyncrasies of authenticity,
Accepting all that you deserve.

A birthing of an imperfect relationship,
Growing together in blissful harmony,
Compromising at the meeting junctions of personalities,
Maturing into the empathetic half of the whole,
Learning the minute breaths of connectivity.

One day at a time, expanding the locked chambers of a
heart,
Once shuttered, shattered and blistered,
Turning the brokenness into loving stability,
For that one worthy of the work,
The loving partner earned within the beating of a wild
dependability.

Love Lives Forever
Once the Bitterness and Anger
Dissipate

Another year wondering if you are happy within your world,
Has life treated you well and has it gone to plan?
Do you understand that within my heart, you are alive and
well?
Just as I remember back when you and I began.

Our love was never truly lost,
Instead, it's locked up tight in a safe and happy place,
One where I go to visit every now and again,
So that I can once more gaze upon your face.

All our happy memories reside deep within my heart,
The nights of loving, the deep conversation, your touch,
Buried deep within my memories, preciously guarded,
Visited as the need arises, remembered as such.

Years have passed, but the memories never dim,
I can close my eyes and feel the love we felt,
The reminders enough to get me through the bad days,
Lucky back then with the hand we were dealt.

I'm honoured to have met you when I did,
The connection instantaneous as I caught your eye,

The years that followed, with no regrets,
Even with the sadness of that final goodbye.

Would you do it all again if given the chance?
Absolutely, there's no hesitation in my response,
Knowing the painful ending that was to follow,
I'd happily shrug my shoulders in nonchalance.

All good things eventually come to an end,
All bad things, too, shall pass,
We certainly had the most dramatic ups and downs,
But would you do it again, I ask?

Love is never truly lost,
As I hold you within my heart,
Yes, it's tough to say that final goodbye,
The sorrow monumental when we part.

But each day that passes, the pain lessens,
Until all that's left is the love we shared,
The anger, the bitterness, dissipates,
But we never lose the fact we once cared.

We were together when the time was right,
We parted when it was meant to be,
We learned our lessons, imparted our wisdom,
And walked away when it was time to be free.

I send you forgiveness and gratitude,
For the love and time you had to give,
Those few years that were solely ours,
For the love in which we got to live.

A Mother's Love
Your Never-Ending Home

You captured her heart before that first meet,
When only the very idea of you was first known,
Her heart was given freely for you to do with as you wish,
Although she already knew you were only on loan.

From that point on, you got to experience,
All that a mother's love entails,
Not a day goes by, not a thing you could do,
To cause a mother's love to ever fail.

A mother's love is an island,
A safe port in any storm,
An unconditional love
You soon learned was the norm.

A mother's love will become your safe haven,
A place to stop and rest your weary feet,
The distance and miles don't mean a thing
When life decides to turn up the heat.

A mother's love will forgive you anything,
No matter what you were to do or say,
A mother's love will see her break her own heart,

Rather than allow you to lose your way.

A mother's love will see her end her own life
To keep you sure and safe,
A mother's love just needs calling,
At any time, situation, or place.

A mother's love doesn't end, ever,
Not when you are born or even all grown,
A mother's love is your surety and security,
Your never-ending home.

Picture of a Love Wasted Drawn After Our Love Had Gone Cold

Please draw me a picture of starlight and space,
Then, capture in detail the look on your face,
Move your pencil across the paper to show your smile
That encompasses the love we had for a while.

Highlight the tears on my face in red and white,
All due to the harsh words spoken that night,
Erase or scribble out the time we spent together,
Blacken the fights that caused stormy weather.

Shade in the happiness with colours so bold,
Include all the heartbreak that turned our love cold,
Show me this picture of our love wasted,
That captures all the pain we have since tasted.

Leave the picture behind as you turn away,
As a reminder of the reasons you wouldn't stay,
Hold the memory of me crying as you left,
Knowing you are the reason I'm feeling bereft.

The Closing of a Chapter
Necessary but Painful

It starts in the chest, a dull ache,
A heart that is running its own race,
As it sinks of its very own accord,
Toughen up, grieve at your own pace.

Regrets, live with each and every one,
Trying to learn the necessary lessons,
Not all is bad; there's some good to see,
Although I'm not proud of some of my confessions.

Missing, pining, a different outcome,
Too late now, the race has been run,
It was short and sweet, devastating,
Although, there were parts that were even fun.

Dreams, wishes, hopes and desires,
All experienced at one time or another,
The good is written in stone and mortar,
Memories and feelings for the other.

Tales woven in magic and grace,
A part of life to never be forgotten,
Carried buried deep within my heart,

Little nuances tried and begotten.

One day, we will remember fondly,
Not yet; it's way too soon and new,
Private thoughts tormented,
Replacements, we've both a few.

I'd love to talk some more one day,
Learn, educate, mischievous play,
I would listen to all you had to say,
We'll both survive and finish okay.

At night, I vividly view and remember,
No escaping my real-life dreams,
You never did feel as you promised,
You quit regularly, or so it seems.

Our time is lost, never to be again,
I'm thankful you cut off all hope,
You severed it quickly, one swift cut,
Giving me the tools needed to cope.

Remember, one day, the possibility,
The outcome and our potential,
Discarded as easily as the bath water,
Pain immediate and consequential.

The Circle of Friendship
The Welcoming Bond

There's not a season, a celebration, a loss, or a heartbreak,
That you don't turn to your circle of friends for comfort and cheer,
Those awesome somebodies that are there for you, always,
In good times and bad, they are the ones you hold dear.

They'll stand by your side in support of your vows,
Watching you grow from singleness to duality,
They hold you tight when you fear the fall,
Of a loved one's loss of mortality.

They laugh at your mistakes, teasing time and time again,
Never allowing you to forget the times of immaturity and silliness,
They reminisce often on your drunken dates,
And guard your back in times of battle and cunning wiliness.

They'll pick you up when you are down,
Lifting you in times of common need,
Administrating emotional stability and compassion,
Whenever your heart is broken, they'll stem the bleed.

Special occasions are all the better,

As they share the graciousness of growing older,
Watching as you grow to be the best version of you,
With their guidance, their support and their comforting shoulder.

The love of friendship is one that allows individuality,
Acceptance is a powerful key,
The rides of your ups, your downs and the flow of life,
The sharing of your true authenticity.

The joy of returning their love and support,
As you offer back the friendship favour,
Just a phone call away at any given time,
Is a lifeline we hold dearly and a comfort we savour.

Life without a circle of friends,
Is a difficult life and a mournful waste,
A lonely existence,
That leaves an unpleasant aftertaste.

The circle of friendship is a blessing,
A gift to all within its beautiful enclosure,
A powerful tethering of love, support, strength and happiness,
To all lucky enough to experience the bonding from friendship's exposure.

She Survived Your Destruction Leaving You Begging on Your Knees

Tears fall from her doe-like eyes as she watches in sadness,
Her heart tearing itself ragged against her chest bone,
Devastation like she's never known, not in her lifetime,
Draining the excitement from her future, leaving a dull monotone.

You set your sights on her total destruction,
Holding tight to the truth as only you know it to be,
You don't believe in fairness, in empathetic reasoning,
Determined to destroy her and then walk away free.

She has you believing in your newfound strength,
Bolstered your well-being until you are blinded by your pride,
The end is near; you treasure the heartlessness of it all,
While you undermine her pity as you cast her aside.

The intensity of your betrayal flourishes your love of drama,
Watching in stony silence as she sobs and bleeds,
Raw emotion, destructive agony, the depth of her misery,
Rewards you in your endeavour as a forbidden man of deeds.

Once you are certain she is broken beyond repair,
You swoop in with loving arms and a tender word,
Calming her fears, distracting her from the worst of her
hysterics,
Passing off her pain as unnecessary and absurd.

You leave her confused and utterly bewildered,
Convincing her of her destiny into impeding insanity,
Manipulating her worries into the realms of her imagination,
Knowing she's innocent, instead, it reeks of your
inhumanity.

She sleeps hoping the darkness will dissipate by morning,
And if not, she begs for the end, the depth of endless sleep,
She gives up; her labouring strength has left her exhausted,
In the agony of your abandonment in which she's left to
weep.

She freely gives you her love, her total adoration,
Worships you in every way in an attempt to give you peace,
But you insist on self-sabotaging your very existence,
Although you refuse to grant her a sacrificial release.

It's only when you realise it's all too little too late,
That you beg for forgiveness, a second chance,
Suddenly, it's you that's living in a world of disbelief,
When you become the creature of circumstance.

Now you sit with your heart broken and your head hung in
shame,

When she serves you her comeuppance, her brewing retaliation,
Politely served with a graceful smile and a twinkle in her eye,
And you realise you're beaten, much to your frustration.

She insists you dine on her revenge until you've received your just desserts,
Promising she'll disappear once you're beaten black and blue,
Her darkness has mated with your retribution,
And she's here to stay until she's seen it through.

Beaten at your own game,
You were a master at the lessons you taught,
And she was a student of sheer perfection,
Excelling at the combatting destruction you wrought.

Near the very end of her harrowing retribution,
She feathers tiny kisses upon your distraught and downcast face,
Then turns and strides confidently through the door,
Satisfied she's brought you to your knees, a well-deserved disgrace.

Love for an Awe-Inspiring Stranger As They Beat Back Life's Constant Obstacles and Come Out On Top

It's with a bleeding, aching heart that I watch,
A total stranger struggles to overcome adversity,
I feel this incessant need to hold them close,
Sheltering them until they land on their feet.

I dream of watching them as they succeed,
Knowing the inner strength it takes to do so,
They fall, but never for long; they're determined,
Not to be beaten and never, ever to give up.

My dream would be to shield them from the blows,
Because life is going to test them to their limits,
Tears fill my eyes; there's so much I want to do,
To help them rise to the occasion, they're a winner.

I want to tell them to continue to hang in there,
My confidence strengthened as I watch in awe,
As they once more stand up, stand tall, head high,
With nothing left but the pride on their face.

They've been kicked, bullied, spat on by life,
But they continue to fight for their dreams,

With nothing left but the love in their heart,
Fighting, never taking no as the final answer.

I am filled with so much hurt and sorrow as I watch,
Wanting, no, needing, to take on their pain,
Knowing they don't deserve the misfortunes,
They've experienced this throughout their short lives.

I need to turn away, the pain in my chest suffocating,
Wishing I could fix it all, change their circumstances,
The injustice of it all, they shouldn't have to fight so hard,
To live their dreams, to succeed in their goals, to live life.

Tears course through the saddened tracks on my face,
My heart swelling with love for an awe-inspiring stranger,
As they beat the odds, miraculously overcoming,
All that is barring their way as they rise up and win.